Metal Detecting Tips

How to Metal Detect for Beginners

David Cardwell

Metal Detecting Tips
by David Cardwell

ISBN 978-0-9866426-2-3

Printed in the United States of America

Latest books by Psylon Press:

100% Blonde Jokes
R. Cristi
ISBN 978-0-9866004-1-8

Choosing a Dog Breed Guide
Eric Nolah
ISBN 978-0-9866004-5-6

Best Pictures Of Paris
Christian Radulescu
ISBN 978-0-9866004-8-7

Best Gift Ideas For Women
Taylor Timms
ISBN 978-0-9866004-4-9

Contents

Introduction   5
Metal Detecting Equipment   7
  Types of Metal Detecting   12
  Metal Detector Features   16
  Other Equipment   18
How to Use your Metal Detector   21
  Basic Adjustments   22
  Hunting in Trashy Areas   26
  How to Use the Right Swing   27
  Using a Pinpointer   29
How to Get Started Making Finds   31
  Beach Detecting   35
  Saltwater Beach Detecting   37
Researching Sites   41
  Map Research   43
  Obtaining Older Maps   45
  Interviews   47
  Photographs   48
  Doing Research on Foot   49
  Roadways   51
  Stone Walls   54
  Wildlife Trails   55
  First Growth Trees   55
  Vegetation and Plants   56
  Structures   56
  Historical Markers   57
Legal Matters   59
  United States Government Property   62
Ideas for Sites to Search   65
Obtaining Permission to Hunt on Private
Property   72
Sample Permission Letter   75
Liability Waiver Form   76
Glossary of Terms   77

Introduction

Metal detecting can be a rewarding hobby that not only brings a tremendous amount of pleasure but can also provide you with the opportunity to unearth an array of treasures. If you have been considering getting involved with metal detecting, you will find that there is much to enjoy about this hobby as well as much to learn, including the right type of equipment to purchase for the type of metal detecting that you would like to engage in, the proper way to search a site and some basic rules and guidelines to keep in mind when locating items hidden beneath the ground.

In this guide we are going to address all of those issues so that you will be able to hit the ground running and get started having fun with metal detecting right away.

Let's get started!

Chapter 1

An Introduction to Metal
Detecting Equipment

One of the most frequent questions that many people new to the idea of metal detecting have about the hobby is which metal detector is best to get started with. If you are thinking of purchasing a metal detector, there are a few factors to keep in mind when choosing your equipment.

The first factor that should be considered is your experience with metal detecting. Have you used a metal detector in the past? If this is to be your first metal detector and you have not used one in the past, think about whether you would prefer a detector that is top of the line that has all of the features so that you can make use of them as you gain experience or whether you would prefer to start out with something simple and then move on to an advanced detector as you gain experience.

You should also think about the amount of time that you plan to devote to metal detecting. This is actually quite important because if you plan to spend a lot of time on your new hobby then you may find that you will do better with a metal detector that has several features. If you only plan to go metal detecting on the weekends and do not plan to spend a lot of time at this hobby then it may not make much sense to you to invest a lot of money in the purchase of a metal detector at this point. Keep in mind; however, that many people have found that once they begin metal detecting they actually end up spending more time on their hobby than they had planned originally.

Budget is also a consideration for many people. The price of many metal detectors is often closely associated with the number and types of features the metal detector includes. A basic beginner metal detector will be able to provide you with plenty of opportunities for locating exciting relics, but if you think you might spend quite a bit of time on your hobby you could quickly be in the market for a new metal detector with advanced features.

When considering the amount of money that you plan to budget for the purchase of your metal detector, you should also keep in mind that you will need to budget for accessories for your metal detector as well, including items such as sand scoops, headphones with volume control, diggers, coils, etc.

In addition, you should consider where you will primarily be using your metal detector before you actually make a purchase. This is important because there are different types of metal detectors which are designed for detecting in certain environments. For instance, some metal detectors are best for searching for items such as jewelry and coins.

Other metal detectors are designed specifically for use on the beach or in water. The difference between the two basic types of metal detectors is that one type contains a meter display for use on land. A beach detector will not have this type of feature, but is designed to be safely operated in

wet conditions.

You should also think about whether you plan to look for gold or silver. Different types of metal detectors feature frequencies that can make locating metal much easier, although you will often need to ground balance these detectors for the best results. In addition, there are metal detectors that are designed for locating items even at significant depths.

Types of Metal Detecting

What type of metal detecting is most interesting to you? Here are a few of the most common types of metal detecting:

Coin Shooting

Coin shooting is a type of metal detecting that is considered to be a specialty. This form of metal detecting typically involves searching for older silver and gold coins.

Relic Hunting

This type of metal detecting involves looking for historic items like military buttons, metals, munitions, etc.

Gold Prospecting

Many people like to use their metal detector to look for items such as gold nuggets. This form of metal detecting is quite popular in the Southwest.

Beach Hunting

This form of metal detecting typically involves walking along the beach to look for items like coins and jewelry that might have been lost by people while on the beach.

Treasure Hunting

This form of metal detecting is primarily restricted to areas where shipwrecks are thought to have occurred. The Florida Keys is one of the most popular locations for treasure hunting due to the number of shipwrecks that have occurred in the area over the years.

Scuba Detecting

This form of metal detecting typically involves the use of scuba diving equipment along with a metal detector in order to look for items in deeper water.

Water Hunting

This type of metal detecting usually involves wading out into the shallow water to locate items; commonly jewelry.

Many people find when they first start out with metal detecting that they want to experiment with many different types of detecting. If that is the case, there are actually many types of metal detectors that will function in a variety of environments, but you should keep in mind that these metal detectors are usually going to be more expensive than a metal detector that is meant for only one environment.

Another factor to take into consideration is your physical shape. If you study a few detectors you will find that there are various configurations and designs available. Some metal detectors are designed to be hung from the waist. If you are going to be detecting for several hours at a time, you want to focus on finding a metal detector that will be comfortable to carry around and use for extended periods of time.

You should also understand that there are three basic types of metal detectors. They are pulse detectors, motion detectors and multi-frequency detectors. If you plan to use your metal detector in land or on fresh water, a detector with motion detection is a good choice, but if you are going to use it in salt water, you would do better to choose a pulse detector. Multi-frequency metal detectors are without a doubt the most expensive option, but provide the benefit of offering a larger range of options.

What about waterproofing? A land detector usually provides many features that can be helpful such as what you may have found before you actually start digging. The built-in display will offer information regarding the type of material that has been found as well as the depth at which the item is located. These are features that will not be included on a waterproof machine, but with a waterproof machine you can use it in shallow water without any safety concerns.

For most people, the final decision of what type of metal detector to buy usually comes down to a matter of budget and how much time you think you will spend using your metal detector versus what you can afford to spend. Do remember that if you buy a metal detector that is very inexpensive, you likely will not be able to penetrate the ground very deeply which means that you probably will not be able to locate many items and that can be disappointing and often result in giving up metal detecting.

On the other hand, if you are able to spend slightly more money you will be able to purchase a more reliable machine that will really open up the world of metal detecting for you. Before long you will be on your way to locating some really great finds; many of which could easily pay for the cost of your metal detector.

Many people are so excited and anxious to get started with metal detecting that they rush into the process of buying a metal detector without giving it any proper thought and consideration. As a result, they often come to regret their purchase. No matter how excited you may be, the best way to approach purchasing a metal detector is to take your time and do the research that is necessary so you can find the detector that will meet your needs.

Metal Detector Features

Let's review some of the more common features that can be included in many metal detectors today.

Depth

This feature refers to the amount of depth that is detectable for a particular metal detector. The amount of depth can depend on the size and the material of a particular item as well as the composition of the soil.

Target

Most of the metal detectors on the market today utilize a visual, tactile or audio alert to let the user know when the detector has picked up a signal. Machines that are less expensive will often use a beep tone that remains the same regardless of what has been detected. A more expensive metal detector will offer distinctive tones that change based on the material that has been detected.

Ground Balance

The minerals that are contained within the earth can effect metal detecting. To help combat this problem many metal detectors offer the ability to adjust for or cancel out those metals to avoid error alerts. Cheaper metal detectors provide a manual adjustment while more expensive machines use microprocessors to automatically handle this.

Detection Mode

Many brands of metal detectors offer users the ability to change settings based on whatever it is they are looking for, such as jewelry mode, relic mode, coin mode, etc.

Sensitivity

Some metal detectors make it possible to adjust the level of sensitive so that the machine is more or less sensitive to particular objects. This can be helpful if you are searching in an area where you know there is a lot of trash such as aluminum.

Display

A higher-end metal detector will typically provide more information on the display than a less expensive machine, such as battery life, target depth, etc.

Other Equipment

Pinpointers

Pinpointer probes can be helpful when you need to look for items while you are digging. The real purpose of this tool is to cut down on the amount of time that you need to spend in recovering items. A probe is actually a lot like a small metal detector. There are two types of pinpointers; inline and handheld. An inline pinpointer probe can be attached to your metal detector. A handheld is a separate device that you hold in your hand.

Coils

Along with the coil that comes standard with your metal detector, there are also other coils that can be used as well including different sizes to help you fine tune your metal detecting efforts. A larger coil may help you to gain more depth but only if the targets you are looking for are larger. A larger coil often will not be able to pick up a small target. You should also remember that a large coil can create some problems with masking. This occurs when there are both good targets and junk targets located directly beneath the coil. If the targets are really close together the junk target may not be canceled out of the search and it is possible that the detector will not pick up the good target at all.

A smaller coil makes it possible to concentrate the signal on the detector, which makes it even more sensitive to looking for smaller targets, but the trade-off is that you will lose some depth.

Headphones

It is a good idea to use headphones no matter where you are searching so that you will not disturb other people with the beeps and tones on your metal detector. If you are going to be looking in an area where there is likely to be a lot of noise, it is especially important to use headphones because you might otherwise miss your metal detector's signal. The best types of headphones will offer adjustable volume control and ear cushions.

Diggers

A digger can help you to excavate the hole where you have located a target item. Many people try to dig out the target with their hands when they are first starting, which can actually be dangerous if there is broken glass in the soil. A digger can help you to safely dig out the target. Diggers are also helpful for excavating soil that is dry and hard.

Scoops

Scoops are ideal to use in soil that is dry and loose, such as on a beach area so that you can easily sort through the soil without worrying about losing any small items.

Chapter 2

How to Use your Metal Detector

Once you have purchased your first metal detector you will likely be anxious to get started with it and head out to begin searching for finds. Before you do that, it is important to make sure you understand the basics of using your metal detector.

Basic Adjustments

To ensure that you are able to get the most from your metal detector you should understand the various adjustments that can be made and how to benefit from them.

Discrimination

Even a basic metal detector will usually have a mode for discrimination. A metal detector works by using a unique phase shift from particular metal objects that result in the signal you hear when an item is targeted. Consequently, you can make adjustments to your metal detector that will make it possible to classify certain types of objects and discriminate between them.

For instance, if you locate an aluminum pull-tab it will have a phase shift that is smaller than that of a silver dime. This means that you can set your metal detector to only beep when a dime is found but not when there is a pull-table. Many metal detectors also give you the option to identify the target that has been found on the display or meter. This type of adjustment can be quite beneficial when you are looking in a location that tends to have a lot of trash.

It should be kept in mind that you may lose some sensitivity when using the discrimination mode for items that are small or deep.

Notch Discrimination

Another form of discrimination is known as notch discrimination. This option allows your metal detector to discriminate and respond only to items that are located within a specific range. At the same time, it will reject items that are above that range. With this option you could set your metal detector to pick up rings and nickels to have it reject pull tabs and screw caps. More expensive machines will usually have adjustment capabilities that are more sophisticated and may even offer a variety of different ranges.

Ground Balance

As previously discussed, soil has a variety of different types of minerals and traces of metal. Some soils contain more of one type of metal than others. For instance, some soil is very high in iron. In some instances, the minerals found in soil may have conductive properties; which means that the signal received by your metal detector could actually arise from the soil rather than an actual object in the soil. You certainly would not want to spend hours searching a site only to discover that the metal detector was picking up the soil and not an object; which is why ground balancing is important.

The ground balance feature makes it possible to compensate for the presence of minerals in the soil. You can adjust the metal detector to ensure that the output of the device will remain consistent. When your metal detector is accurately balanced you will be able to pinpoint the site of a prospective target with far greater precision as well as more accurately estimate the depth of the target.

Different metal detectors have different techniques for ground balancing. The most basic feature is usually a knob that allows you to raise or lower the loop on the detector. You can continue to do this until you achieved the ideal ground balance. This can become somewhat tedious; however, which is why higher-end metal detectors offer an automatic ground balancing feature. There are also even more sophisticated metal detectors that provide a gradual ground balancing feature that changes as the composition of the soil changes. This feature is known as Tracking Ground Balance. The main advantage it provides is that after you have balanced your metal detector you will not have to worry about it again for the rest of the day.

Sensitivity

No matter whether your metal detector is basic or advanced; most units do provide a sensitivity adjustment that will allow you to adjust how sensitive the machine is to metals within the ground and other objects. For instance, if you are looking in an location that has a lot of trash you may find this feature to be beneficial.

Visual Discrimination Indication

Some metal detectors also offer a visual discrimination indicator mode that allows you to make better informed decisions regarding whether to dig for an object.

Non-Motion and Motion

Ground balance may not be enough in some cases. For instance, if the signal that the machine receives from the soil is much stronger than that from the target, the ground signal will often remain the same or change only at a slow rate as you move the loop. The target signal will sharply rise and then go away as you move the loop over it. Consequently, it can be helpful to have a way of separating the ground signal from the target signal. This can be accomplished by monitoring the rate of change instead of the actual signal. This is where motion modes come in.

Audio Threshold

This feature makes it possible for you to adjust the sound of the hum that is produced when your metal detector is operating. Everyone has different levels of hearing, so this is an important feature. If you opt to use headphones that have an adjustment feature, you may want to tune the audio threshold louder and then use the volume controls on the headphone to adjust it to a fainter sound.

Hunting in Trashy Areas

We have talked quite a bit about areas that contain a lot of trash such as pull-tabs, aluminum foil, screw caps, etc. It can be frustrating to search in these areas because your metal detector may continually produce signals when it picks up trashy items rather than items of any real significant meaning. That does not mean that you should completely rule out searching in these areas because there are some things you can do to make it more successful and less frustrating.

For example, you can try switching a smaller coil. Using a larger coil in an area with a lot of trash is usually going to end in frustration. A smaller coil will be an investment but if you are going to be spending a lot of time with your metal detecting hobby, it can be worth it, especially when searching in areas that have a lot of trash.

Make sure that you have ground balanced your metal detector in an area that is fairly clean before you begin looking in the trashy area. You may also need to lock the ground tracking on your metal detector as well; if your machine has that capability. Also, take care to adjust the sensitivity on the metal detector so that you will be able to have a good amount of depth while also maintaining stability.

It is also a good idea to use a slower swing speed when searching in a trashy area using a small coil. If you go too fast you are likely to miss items. Keep in mind that it can take some practice, time and patience when searching in areas that has a lot of trash. You need to become accustomed to the various sounds that your machine will produce. Once you have spent some time practicing you may be surprised at just how many great finds you can come across even in trashy areas.

How to Use the Right Swing

Practice truly does make a world of difference in successful using your metal detector. You will need to spend some time becoming accustomed your particular brand of metal detector. Each one is different and you need to become well acquainted with your machine. You will also need to spend some time practicing your swing. Swing is the way in which you move your metal detector, particularly the coil, over the search area. If you move your machine too rapidly you will probably miss out on some items. If you keep the coil raised too high you might also miss out on important items.

The most basic swing technique is known as sweeping. This is the first technique that you should work on mastering. It involves moving the coil side to side over the ground. Be aware that swinging the detector back and forth is likely not going to produce good results. You need to be sure that you are using an overlapping swing to a slight degree so that you will not accidentally overlook anything.

Also, take care that your swing is level to the ground. Many people new to the hobby make the mistake of bringing the coil in a slightly upward location while moving it side to side. This may cause you to lose out on some sensitivity and miss items.

Furthermore, you need to be certain that you are actively listening for the signals while you are sweeping with your machine. It can be easy to miss faint signals, especially when you are just starting out. A common mistake is to dig only for items that produce loud signals. Even a faint signal can be an indicator of a good find beneath the ground. Time and practice will help you to become accustomed to listening for those fainter signals and what they mean.

Using a Pinpointer

Previously we discussed the benefits of using a pinpointer after you have located an item with your metal detector. The real benefit of a pinpointer is that it can help you to be more precise in pinpointing the precise location of an object. Beginners will find a pinpointer to be particularly helpful. To use this tool, you need to dig out the plug in the ground and then place the pinpointer into the hole. Be sure that the tuner control has been adjusted and then turn on the pinpointer and begin scanning the target area. You should receive a signal that will offer information to help you in determining whether the item is located at a further depth or if you need to look more toward the side of the hole.

Chapter 3

How to Get Started Making Finds

After you have identified a particular spot where you would like to search for items, you will need to dig out the item. There is a procedure that should be used when digging out items in order to help minimize damage to both the property as well as the item.

- Begin by pushing the digger into the soil. Push the digger in to a depth of about 4" to allow you to get beneath any grass roots. Keep in mind that you will need to try to limit damage as much as possible.

- The next step is to cut out a grass plug in a semi-circle shape. Pry up the plug of grass so that there is a hinge left on one side that is not cut. This will make it easier to replace the plug when you are finished searching.

- Use a bandana or handkerchief or some other type of cloth that you can drop the soil into. This will help to prevent littering the soil over the rest of the grass.

- Next, take the coil of your metal detector and pass it over the soil that you have piled onto the cloth. This should let you know whether you have dug deeply enough and whether the target item is now in the plug or whether you should dig deeper.

- After locating the target item and removing it from the dirt, take the drop cloth back to the hole and place the dirt back inside the hole. Make sure that you have tamped the dirt down firmly.

- Flip the plug back into the hole. The grass should be facing upward.

- Next, lightly press the grass plug so that it is level with the surrounding area. After you have finished it should not be detectable that you have disturbed the area at all.

Beach Detecting

Beaches are a great place to look for many different items and are great for beginners. While you also have the opportunity to enjoy sunshine and the scenery you will also find that you have a great chance to locate a number of different items that are commonly lost along the beach while people are jogging, sunbathing or simply enjoying the sights.

When detecting on the beach you should not be surprised to find that there are other people detecting as well. Beaches are extremely popular for detecting. It is not that uncommon to see perhaps half a dozen people on the beach with their metal detectors. When there are other people out searching, you should try to be discrete about what you are doing because you certainly do not want to alert others to the fact that you may have found something interesting.

In most instances, individuals engaged in metal detecting as a hobby are great, honest folks, there are always a few people who are only involved in the hobby for what they can find, which means that it is important to use some caution when you are searching on the beach to be sure that you do not experience any problems.

There are some techniques that you can use to improve your chances of finding something while you are out searching on the beach, in spite of the number of people who are often out searching on beaches today. First, try searching on beaches that are less crowded. This will ensure that you will have far less competition and may be able to find more items.

When using your metal detector be sure to keep an eye on how high your coil is situated. If you have it about a foot above the ground you are likely going to miss out on a lot. Many people, especially when they are first starting out, make the mistake of holding the coil too high off the ground because they are concerned about damaging the coil. This is a valid concern but the simple fact is that you are not going to find a lot if you go about it this way and that, of course defeats the entire purpose of what you are trying to accomplish.

There are also certain times that tend to be better for searching on the beach than other times. The weekends and holidays tend to be the most crowded times for beaches. Sunday evenings are often the best times to head to the beach because you can often look for items without a lot of people being there and also may be able to look for items that were lost when the crowds were there over the weekend.

Saltwater Beach Detecting

When you are searching in water and on the beach, bear in mind that you will need to use equipment that is somewhat different than what should be used when searching on dry land. Some metal detectors are waterproof up to a certain point, but in most instances a dry land metal detector is not entirely waterproof. Along with a waterproof metal detector, if you are going to search on the beach and in water you will also need a special water scoop as well as a waterproof hunting pouch for holding the items you find.

Perhaps one of the biggest differences between hunting on dry land and on the beach is that the sand that is on the beach is continually on the move; which is usually not the case on dry land. The appearance of the beach can change based on the wind, currents and tide. If you do not visit the beach often you might not notice these changes because they can occur gradually but if you go frequently you might be much more observant regarding even slight changes that might have taken place.

You should also keep in mind that the amount of time that is available to you to search on saltwater beaches will be limited by the tides. This is why it is important to take advantage of the amount of time that is available and begin your searches in areas where there is less sand. Sweep the area with your metal detector first and focus on finding good signals so that you can then better concentrate your search. Look for areas where there are more pebbles and sand than in other areas. This is a good way to find areas where the sand may have been moved, which can often be a good indication of a channel location. In areas where the sand has been moved you will be more likely to locate some good finds.

You should also time your searches on saltwater beaches in order to achieve the best results as well. During the summer will usually prove to be most effective because the water will not be as cold. Furthermore, you may find that your searches are more effective in the mornings, primarily because the water will be calmer during these times.

You can often find some excellent sites to search by watching the tide so try to obtain a tide chart for the local area where you will be searching. This can assist you in finding areas that can be good to search once the sands have moved along with the tides.

One of the more common problems that many people run into when using their metal detector on a beach is that they often do not dig deeply enough to reach the items that have been targeted by the metal detector. When searching on dry land you may find that items that are buried quite deep may just be trash but that is sometimes different on the beach. Trash items like screw caps are usually going to be located right at the top of the surface on a beach.

If you are searching and finding a lot of trash, you are probably not looking in the right area and should instead move deeper out into the water. You should also keep in mind that in many cases gold items are not going to be located directly on the sand; not unless it was recently lost. Generally you will find gold items right beneath the sand so make sure you are prepared to search at a greater depth in order to find items of value such as gold items.

The best way to achieve optimal results when searching on a beach near saltwater is to spend plenty of time practicing. When you search on a saltwater beach it is going to be somewhat different than searching on dry land or on a freshwater beach; which means that you need to spend some time to become accustomed to the differences you will encounter. Give yourself plenty of time and have patience. It is always possible that you might go home without finding anything, if you spend time practicing and hit a spot that is rife with good finds all of the time you have spent searching will have been well worth it.

Also, keep in mind that while you are searching on the beach there are few matters of courtesy or etiquette that should be followed.

Always show courtesy and respect to others. When you search on dry land you should cover any holes that you make and that is the same when searching on the beach. Remember that jogging on the beach is a popular activity and you certainly do not want anyone to stumble over a hole that you did not properly cover. You do not want to be responsible for causing anyone to experience an injury.

Keep in mind as well that you should try not to hunt at night. This is actually more a matter of safety rather than courtesy. Some people do choose to hunt at night but in most instances you will find that you will not be able to see anything and there is always the chance of running into something dangerous because you cannot see it.

Chapter 4

Researching Sites

There are many different areas where you can search for some great relics and other items such as at the beach and parks, but many of the best places where you can search for items are actually off the beaten path. This is often especially true when it comes to historical finds and relics. Many individuals have found excellent items in areas that might at first look as though they would not be at all important.

To locate these places you will need to be in some time researching to scout potential locations, including research old maps. In order to achieve optimal results, it is a good idea to carefully consider what it is that you are hoping to find; otherwise it can be hard to research all of the proper facts you will need.

First, give some thought to identifying potential sites. These sites are usually going to be places that have been significantly used over time. How will you know how much a site has been used? The only way is through research.

In addition to looking at maps you will also need to spend some time on the ground actually going over the site. It might seem as though these methods would take a lot of time but they are actually activities that can be put to good use during the colder months of the year when you would not usually be out using your metal detector anyway. By getting in some research time during the winter months you will be that much further ahead when warmer weather arrives and you are ready to head outside with your metal detector.

Map Research

Let's begin by looking at how to conduct map research. Being able to read and understand a map is critical in treasure and relic hunting. You should be able to accurately read new topographical maps as well as the older maps that were produced years ago. The goal behind this activity is to be able to have access to a variety of older maps for the target location you are interested in searching. After you have access to a number of maps you can then compare them to newer topographical maps and see how that particular site might have changed over time.

You should be prepared for the fact that reading older maps can sometimes be challenging. Maps from a long time ago are often known as plats rather than maps. Spending some time becoming familiar with them can be an excellent use of your time and can certainly aide your search efforts in the future.

While reading plats, keep in mind that these maps are not usually drawn to scale. Consequently, the detail that you would typically see on newer maps is usually not going to be present on an older map. It should also be understood that township maps were not usually issued until around the middle part of the 19th century. Fortunately, many local libraries and state archives often have these maps. In some instances you may even be

able to locate them online, which can certainly be convenient.

You will actually find that there is often a wealth of information that is available from looking at these old maps. For instance, you might discover the location of schools and old homesteads. Generally, the names of landowners will be marked, although it might only be a first initial and last name. Even so, that can often provide you with an excellent clue, particularly when comparing several maps over a long period of time.

In addition, there are also many other maps that can be beneficial including military maps, tax maps, property deeds, census records, etc.

Obtaining Older Maps

As you begin looking for older maps, it helps to have an understanding of why and when these maps were produced. It is often the case with older maps, which were sometimes also known as land ownership maps, that they were produced for property assessment. In some cases they were also used to attract new settlers to that particular area.

One of the wonderful things about older maps is that they can really provide you with some great insight into the population of that region at that particular time. In this way they can provide you with some great clues if you are looking for relics. You might even be able to locate towns that have been forgotten for quite some time.

Original maps were frequently produced originally as large wall maps; reaching up to around six feet in height. A variety of survey zones would usually be included on these maps. Many times these maps were categorized based on voter districts, land deeds, political districts, etc. Furthermore, they would often provide information such as the name of the landowner, the amount of acreage owned by that individual and even what type of occupation that landowner was involved in.

You can often obtain these maps through government institutions and libraries, but remember when you are going through these sources that you will usually be on your own because there are often no resources allotted for staff. You might also consider purchasing a map through a library online. This is often a good way to obtain some fairly high quality images. Currently, there are two map libraries that are available online that are often used by metal detector hobbyists. Historic Maps Restored provides map prints for sale that have been digitally re-mastered. They have a fairly good reputation for offering large maps of old mining areas, forts, ghost towns, military installments, stagecoach trails, towns, wagon routes and other areas that have long since vanished from general view because they have become overgrown over time. You can often find quite a bit of detail on these maps including businesses, homes and buildings. Maps of the Past is another great research resource that provides a good selection as well.

Interviews

Another great way to uncover detail about areas and who might have once lived there is to conduct interviews with people who are familiar with that area. Many of the old-timers in the area can provide you with a wealth of information. In fact, you will likely find that you can obtain far more valuable and in-depth information through interviews that you would be able to uncover in any book or map. The most important fact here is that you need to be sure that you have posed the correct questions and then be willing to listen to what the other person has to say. Make sure that you set aside plenty of time for your interviews and do not try to rush them along.

Many older individuals are often very excited whenever anyone takes an interest in what they have to say so it can often seem as though they might be rambling on about something that really has nothing to do with what interests you but you will find that if you allow them to go ahead and just talk that you can uncover very helpful information that you would never have suspected.

When conducting an interview it is a good idea to make sure that you have a tape recorder with you, but always be sure to ask permission before you actually record the interview. This technique will allow you to focus on listening to what the person has to say and not have to constantly write down notes and possibly miss something important in the process.

Finally, always make sure that you show proper respect and deference to the person you are interviewing.

Photographs

Old photographs can also prove to be an excellent resource for the information that you need in order to find excellent sites to search with your metal detector. Along the same lines postcards are another good resource because they can often provide you with a good idea of what an area looked like before modern times.

If you are considering searching an area but you have not been able to pinpoint the exact location of that area, make sure that you try to find some old photographs of that spot. You might have luck in locating such photographs in the genealogical section of your local library. Another good opportunity to find good resources is to attend a local genealogical meeting. These are often held in many areas and can also provide you with excellent sources of resources and connections, including how to locate old trails, settlements and townships.

Keep in mind when you are attending these types of meetings that it may be a good idea not to necessarily reveal exactly what it is that you want to do. While you will certainly need to obtain permission from a landowner to search on private land once you are ready to get started, if you broadcast your interest and intentions during these types of meetings you might find yourself with a big of an argument on your hand. Many people view metal detecting as a wonderful hobby that can also provide you with excellent insight into the past, not everyone feels that way.

Doing Research on Foot

You should also be able to obtain quite a lot of information by doing some research on foot. Many hobbyists prefer to save this type of research for the warmer months; but there are advantages to doing this type of research in the winter as well because you will not have as many leaves blocking structures and making them more difficult to see.

During the colder months of the year you might not be able to actually do a lot with your metal detector, particularly if the ground is frozen, which makes the wintertime an excellent time to begin targeting and scouting potential search sites that you might be interested in searching further in the spring.

Roadways

Roadways often change over time. There may be dirt roads and side paths that can prove to be valuable in your search efforts. Consider the fact that many of the paths that were once used are not in use today and vice versa. Even when it appears that you are just looking at a path that seems to take off through the woods, there is likely a reason that path was there in the first place. Even though it might have been a long time ago that the road or path was used it can still be valuable to your search efforts.

While you are looking for roads remember that the type of road infrastructure that was in use during the 19th century and earlier was actually far different from what we are familiar with today. In many cases, such infrastructure was not actually developed until the mid-19th century and later. Prior to this, roads were often nothing more than just merely a clearing through the middle of the woods.

You may often find that there will even be tree stumps that are left in the middle of such paths. Travel during this time could be extremely hazardous and roads were often rough and bumpy, meaning that stage coaches, carriages and wagons were often forced to shift from side to side in an effort to keep from tipping over. What this means for you is that there is often a good chance that you can find relics and treasures on the remains of these roads left over from items spilling out of various transportation conveyances from days gone by.

Old trails and roadways can sometimes surprise you in regards to the number of coins, relics and other items that they hold. You might even be able to find an entire cache of objects if you are fortunate enough; such as a container with several items of jewelry or coins. One of the main reasons why you might find such a cache is that oftentimes pioneers and settlers would bury their possessions in order to protect them. This was particularly common in rural areas because there were no banks.

Many times settlers would either never retrieve their possessions or just simply forget about this. This could easily happen if a family was forced to move away quickly. They might have thought they would be able to return for the items later but were unable to do so for some reason. On the frontier families were sometimes killed or died from disease and there might have been no one left to come back for the items.

In such cases you may come across excellent finds such as jewelry and coins but it is also fairly common to find weaponry too. If you happen to be a weaponry buff, this is naturally a find that will excite you, especially if you are able to uncover old guns and knives. Such items will commonly be quite rusty so it is usually a good idea to be sure you wear gloves and take extreme care when you retrieve such items.

During this time in history roadways were often made up of different types of materials. The materials used would usually vary from one region to another; with locals using whatever resources were available to them in that area. Crushed oyster shells and crushed corncobs were actually fairly common road paving materials in many areas.

When you are searching out abandoned roads, you will need to keep your mind open and learn to think out the box. This is because abandoned roads may not be immediately visible to you and it can be fairly easy to overlook a road that was once fairly well traveled.

Possible clues that can indicate the presence of a road include:

- Openings in the forest or woods
- Intersections near roads
- Bridge remains
- Areas near creek crossings
- Openings in stone walls
- Side paths that appear to brand off from roadways
- Fruit trees growing near the side of the road or in the woods
- Depressions in the earth near roads or paths
- Plants and vegetation on the side of the road that seem out of place

Stone Walls

You will not find stone walls in every part of the country but they are fairly common in certain areas such as New England. You will often find that parts of stone walls go right through the woods. This could seem somewhat strange when you first see this but when you consider the changes that have occurred over time it actually makes quite a bit of sense. As farmland was cleared over time, many farmers often collected the stones and rocks to establish these walls. As homesteads were sometimes abandoned and the farms became overgrown with the growth of trees, the walls remained.

While searching or stone walls remember that these walls usually were built to divide property and also to keep livestock from wandering off. As you identify stone walls you can often gather quite a bit of information about that particular site. For instance, you might find that an old home once stood on that site by seeing the remains of a cellar; which can prove to be an excellent place to look for treasures and relics. Many people often buried their valuable possessions near walls and sometimes even inside walls.

Wildlife Trails

You may also find wildlife trails to be helpful in locating sites for searching. Many of these trails are located near old home sites and homesteads. It can be easy to overlook these sites because they are often at least partially covered up by woods and other growth. In many instances, these old home sites were abandoned a hundred years or even longer ago. Even so, the wildlife still return to feed off old fruit trees or other types of vegetation that have continued to survive in the area.

First Growth Trees

It can also be helpful to have an understanding of the way the woods develop. Many times, the woods and forests that you see today are actually made up of second and third growth generation trees. Areas that once were farmland and were cleared in order to plant crops were later abandoned and the forests began to reclaim these areas. The vegetation and trees that grew back up in these areas are now the second and sometimes third generation of the original trees and vegetation that were once cleared by those early farmers so long ago.

You can usually spot these areas by walking through the woods and noticing trees that seem to be somewhat different from the others. For example, it might be broader in girth or taller. This can be a good indication that this is a first-growth tree instead of a second or third generation growth tree. Many times frontiersmen and pioneers would leave a tree as a type of marker while clearing all of the others. You might also find a tree stump in an area that is a remainder from a first generation growth which can indicate the presence of an old home site as well.

Vegetation and Plants

Many old home sites frequently contained a variety of different forms of vegetation and growth. This often included various forms of flowers and roses. The farmland would have been planted using different vegetables. Many times there would also be a variety of nut and fruit trees planted on homesteads as well, including cherry trees, apple trees, peach trees, pear trees, pecan trees and chestnut trees. As you explore the woods, especially during the spring when such trees would be blooming, you can often find that hints of these forms of vegetation will remain and can serve as excellent indications that there was once a home in that location.

Structures

You should also make sure you are on the lookout for structures as you explore the woods as well. While you might not find an entire home you could find the remains of a cellar. Sometimes it may be nothing more than a depression in the ground that can provide you with a clue that there was once a cellar in that location. Look for stone slabs as well. These will often seem out of place in the middle of the woods but can provide an excellent basis for researching the area further.

Historical Markers

Throughout the country historical markers are placed in strategic locations to indicate where something important occurred or someone notable lived. While some parts of the country may have more historical markers than others, they can serve as wonderful sources of research. Many of these markers were erected during the early 20th century and can frequently be found in front of forts, camp sites, town squares, churches, battlefield sites, etc.

Chapter 5

Legal Matters

When you are ready to start searching an area, it is imperative that you make sure you understand whether you can legally search in that area or not. While there are not really any laws that prohibit metal detecting, you certainly cannot just go poking around on private property and digging it up. Also, there are some public lands where you might be prohibited from metal detecting as well, particularly if that site has significant historical interest.

It should also be kept in mind that laws can differ between cities, counties and states in regards to public property. While you might be allowed to search on state property in one state that might not be the case in another state so always make sure you do your homework and never make assumptions. To make matters even more confusing you may find that in some state parks you are allowed to search but not in others. Due to the fact that this can be confusing, it is imperative that you take the time to contact the appropriate authority and be sure you have obtained written permission to conduct your search activities.

You should not allow the legal aspect of metal detecting to frighten you or keep you from going out and hunting, but it is important to make sure that you exercise due diligence. There are actually numerous locations where you can go and use your metal detector without encountering any types of problems in most instances. The main thing is to be sure that you are aware of the boundaries and that you have taken the necessary steps to obtain permission before you actually start poking around.

There are a few specific guidelines that should be kept in mind regarding battlefields. Most large battlefield sites are going to be located on federal and sometimes state historic areas. If you try to hunt in these areas you may be subjected to substantial fines and possibly even jail time. This is not the case for all military camp sites, routes and engagement areas because not all of these sites are actually located in state and federal historic parks. Many can actually be found on private property. In many instances, battles took places in locations that were really nothing more than farm or pasture land.

While the layout and the ownership of these lands have changed over the course of history, there are many that have actually remained the same with very few changes. If you are able to locate a possible battle site area that is located in a pasture or some other open area, be sure that you contact the landowner and obtain permission before you attempt to do any hunting. You may be surprised to find that the owner will actually give permission as long as you agree to do any hunting with the area is not in use. Do make sure that you verify property and boundary lines so that you do not accidentally cross over onto someone else's property.

United States Government Property

Prior to making any attempts to hunt on U.S. property it is imperative that you understand whether you can legally detect on these properties based on the Antiquities Act of 1906. In certain circumstances, there are also other laws that can apply.

The Antiquities Act of 1906

The Antiquities Act of 1906 reads in part:

"Be it enacted by the Senate and House of Representatives of the United States of America in Congress assembled, That any person who shall appropriate, excavate, injure, or destroy any historic or prehistoric ruin or monument, or any object of antiquity, situated on lands owned or controlled by the Government of the United States, without the permission of the Secretary of the Department of the Government having jurisdiction over the lands on which said antiquities are situated, shall, upon conviction, be fined in a sum of not more than five hundred dollars or be imprisoned for a period of not more than ninety days, or shall suffer both fine and imprisonment, in the discretion of the court."

The 1966 National Historic Preservation Act

In 1966 the National Historic Preservation Act was passed in order to protect cultural resources. It reads in part:

"This act supplements the provisions of the Antiquities Act of 1906. The law makes it illegal to destroy, excavate or remove information from Federal or Indian lands any archeological resources without a permit from the land manager. Permits may be issued only to educational or scientific institutions and only if the resulting activities will increase knowledge about archeological resources. Regulations for the ultimate disposition of materials recovered as a result of permitted activities state that archeological resources excavated on public lands remain the property of the United States. Archeological resources excavated from Indian lands remain the property of the Indian or Indian tribe having rights of ownership over such resources."

The 1979 Archaeological Resources Protection Act

In 1979 the Archaeological Resources Protection Act was passed in order to provide even more protection. It reads in part:

"The term "archaeological resource" means any material remains of past human life or activities which are of archaeological interest, as determined under uniform regulations promulgated pursuant to this chapter. Such regulations containing such determination shall include, but not be limited to: pottery, basketry, bottles, weapons, weapon projectiles, tools, structures or portions of structures, pit houses, rock paintings, rock carvings, intaglios, graves, human skeletal materials, or any portion or piece of any of the foregoing items. Nonfossilized and fossilized paleontological specimens, or any portion or piece thereof, shall not be considered archaeological resources, under the regulations under this paragraph, unless found in archaeological context. No item shall be treated as an archaeological resource under regulations under this paragraph unless such item is at least 100 years of age.

No person may excavate, remove, damage, or otherwise alter or deface, or attempt to excavate, remove, damage, or otherwise alter or deface any archaeological resource located on public lands or Indian lands unless such activity is pursuant to a permit issued under section 470cc of this title, a permit referred to in section 470cc(h)(2) of this title, or the exemption contained in section 470cc(g)(1) of this title."

While clearly none of these laws make any mention specifically regarding metal detecting, you still must be quite careful when you consider doing any metal detecting on property owned by the United States government, particularly any Native American lands which could potentially be burial grounds.

Ideas for Sites to Search

While this may sound disheartening to you, keep in mind that there are actually still numerous places where you can search, even if you are looking for gold.

Below are some possible ideas:

National Forests
In most instances you can search in national forests provided that you are searching for items that are not 50 years old or older. This rule dates back to the 1979 ARPA which states that you may not hunt for manmade items that are 50 years old or older. You will usually not be allowed to search in historic sites. According to the 1979 ARPA, permits can be obtained but in most cases they are only available to archaeologists.

Other possible sites where you can usually search without any problems include:

- **Town and City Parks** - Even in small parks there are usually items that will have been lost there over time. Such sites are excellent for searching for jewelry and coins.

- **Old Schools** - Jewelry and coins are the most frequent finds in these sites, especially old high school and class rings. Keep in mind that if you do find a ring you should make every attempt to locate the original owner.

- **Old Home Sites** - There are many different items that can be found in old home sites including coins and jewelry as well as various other relics.

- **Old Church Sites** - You can often find old coins in these locations that were most likely lost when collection plates were passed around.

- **Picnic Groves** - During the 19th century picnics were a popular pastime. As a result you are likely to find jewelry and even coins that were lost during such events.

- **Circus and Fair Sites** - Coins and jewelry are also often found in these locations.

- **Summer Camps** - You may be able to find a wide variety items that have been lost in these areas over the years.

- **Scout Camps** - These are good sites to look for coins, medals and other type of relics.

- **Swimming Areas** - These are always excellent sites in which to look for jewelry, coins and other items that people may have lost while swimming.

- **Athletic Fields** - You have a good chance of finding jewelry as well as coins in such fields.

- **Rodeo Arenas** - You can find a variety of different items here ranging from belt buckles to horseshoes to coins and jewelry.

- **Campgrounds** - Look for items such as coins and jewelry. Keep in mind that if the campground is located in a state park you should always obtain permission before hunting.

- **Beaches** - Beaches are an excellent starting point for beginners. The variety of what you can find at beaches is always quite interesting.

- **Ghost Towns** - All over the country, especially in the southwest, there are numerous ghost towns that have been abandoned over the years. You never know what you might find in ghost towns. You could even possibly find some gold nuggets and other treasures.

- **Roadside Rest Stops** - There can be all kinds of things lost in roadside rest stops while people are taking breaks during their travels. These are excellent sites to search.

- **Revival sites** - Revival sites are often much like old church sites. You have a good chance of finding coins that may have been dropped when collections were taken up.

- **Amusement Parks** - Another great site to look for coins and jewelry that may have been lost over the years.

- **Fishing Areas** - In these sites you may be able to find items such as jewelry and coins but also other items such as tackle and lures.

- **Flea Market Areas** - You can find a variety of items in such areas, including artifacts, jewelry and coins.

- **Racetracks** - These are excellent sites to search for coins.

- **Drive-ins** - At one time drive-in movies were quite popular. Today these old sites offer the opportunity to find items like jewelry and coins.

- **Motels** - The parking lots of motels are excellent places to search for jewelry and coins.

- **Farmer's Markets** - Many times coins are dropped during sales transactions in such sites. You may even be able to find old coins if these markets have been around for some time.

- **Hiking Trails** - You can find a variety of items that may have been dropped in these areas over the years.

- **Parking Spots and Lover's Lanes** - You can find items such as jewelry and coins that may have been lost in these areas.

- **Town Squares** - Town squares are often a great place to look or a number of different items, particularly around courthouses.

- **Fence Posts** - It may seem a bit strange today but fence posts were often once used to mark locations of places where people buried valuables. If they are on private property make sure you ask before you begin to hunt.

- **Dance Sites** - Dance sites in rural areas are a great place to look for jewelry and even coins that could have been lost during dances over the years.

- **Bridges** - Bridges and areas where bridges were once located are excellent places to look for a variety of items that could have been lost by travelers throughout history.

- **Ferry Sites** - A wide variety of items were often lost on ferries, making ferry sites a valuable source to search today.

- **Wells** - In the past many items were often dropped down wells on accident but were also sometimes placed them for safekeeping.

- **Old Trash and Dump Sites** - You just never know what you might find in these locations.

- **Outhouses** - This may seem quite strange to you but the remains of an old outhouse could prove to be quite valuable. In some cases people buried items there because they rightly thought that very few people would think to look there!

- **Under Old Porches** - Think of all the things that could have been dropped under a porch or may have even been deliberately put there for safekeeping.

- **Storm Cellars and Basement Steps** - These sites can prove to be valuable sites to search as well.

- **Construction Sites** - These sites are often a good place to look because bulldozers will have done a lot of the work for you already, unearthing years worth of dirty and making it much easier for you to find a variety of items.

Naturally, this list is by no means exhaustive, but it should give you a good idea of the many places where you can begin hunting with your metal detector. Keep in mind that in many cases these sites may already have been searched by others but that does not mean that they have been depleted of good finds. They may not have been searched well and there could still be many great items left to find. Someone may have overlooked items or they might have missed the signals from their metal detector. They might not even have dug deeply enough. Whatever the reason, you should never rule out a site simply because you think someone else might have retrieved all of the good finds before you.

Remember that there are a few areas that you should generally steer away from, including:

- Military reservations
- Native American reservations
- National parks and monuments

Obtaining Permission to Hunt on
Private Property

It is imperative to understand that all property is owned by someone. Even if the land looks as though it may be uninhabited and has been abandoned, it is still owned by someone. If you would like to search on private property you must obtain permission from the landowner. Bear in mind that even if there is not a no trespassing sign posted on the property that does not mean that you can just go hunting around on that property.

Keep in mind as well that everyone in the United States has the right to protect their property. You MUST obtain permission before you enter someone else's property or you may find yourself facing problems. Show courtesy and respect and obtain permission first.

It is always best to obtain written permission rather than verbal permission whenever possible. This will help to ensure there are no misunderstandings later on. The permission document should include information regarding specific times when you can hunt on the property. Along with obtaining permission from the owner of the property you should also make sure you fully address how any finds will be divided with the property owner. Do not just assume that the property owner will let you have everything you find. If you find something valuable they may very well want a portion of it. Even if what you find is only interesting and not necessarily valuable, they may still wish to have a split. If you take the time to address these matters ahead of time you will not have any misunderstandings or problems later on.

One way to obtain the permission you need to hunt on private property is to send a letter to the property owner. This is a much less intrusive manner than simply approaching them in person; which is likely to catch them off-guard and may not provide you with the best results. If you send them a letter you will be able to give them more time to consider your request and you may find that you receive better results and a great chance at obtaining the permission you need.

Be sure that you include your contact information in the letter and if you have not heard anything back from them within about a week you should then follow-up with a telephone call just to be sure that the property owner did indeed receive the letter. You should offer to answer any questions they may have that might help to alleviate possible concerns. Remember that you will not be able to obtain permission from every property owner you approach. If you are not able to obtain permission from a property owner, keep in mind that there are plenty of sites where you can search.

On the following page you will find a sample permission letter that you can send out to property owners to obtain permission to search on private properties.

Sample Permission Letter

Permission to Metal Detect on Privately Owned Property

I, _____

_____ agree to allow _____

_____(insert your name and address), to use a metal detector to search for and recover coins, relics and artifacts that may be buried on my property located at: __

_____

_____ (insert property address). Recovery shall include digging small holes. All holes will be repairs to as close to original condition as possible. The permission I grant in this letter shall remain in effect until I revoke it in writing.

Property Owner

Date

Liability Waiver Form

In consideration for permission to utilize a metal detector to hunt for and recover buried coins, relics and other types of artifacts that are buried on the property located at _____
_____ (insert property address) and owned by
_____(insert name of property owner). I, _____
(insert your name here) agree to release from all liability for personal injury or property damage that I may suffer as a result of the owner's negligence while on the owner's property only during the period and at the time of such search. This release shall be binding and forever discharge _____ ,
his/her heirs, executors, and administrators, from all actions, causes of action, claims and demands for, upon, or by reason of any damage, loss, injury, or suffering which I may sustain while engaged in metal detecting on the owners property.

____   _____

(type your name & address)

Date

Glossary of Terms

Air Test - This term refers to a test that is performed by moving various sizes of metal samples under the metal detector in order to check the target response and features of the metal detector.

All Metal - This term refers to an operating mode which allows acceptance of all types of metals. This type of setting is most commonly used with the Ground Balance mode.

Back Reading - This term refers to a false signal that can occur when a rejected target comes close to contacting the bottom of the metal detector coil.

Bench Test - This term refers to an air test that is used to specifically determine the approximate discrimination setting for different types of metal samples. This setting is commonly used in areas that are non-metallic.

Body Mount - Refers to a type of configuration that makes it possible for the control housing to be separated from the shaft; which can reduce arm fatigue while searching.

Cache - This term refers to a hoard of valuables that was secretly or intentionally buried.

Coil - This term refers to the search coil that is attached to the bottom of the metal detector.

Coin Depth Indicator - This term refers to a visual indicator that is utilized to indicate the depth of items buried; either in inches or millimeters.

Control Housing - This term refers to the box that holds the circuit boards, indicators, power supply and meter on the metal detector.

Drift - This term refers to the loss of tuning stability that can be caused by the battery condition or sometimes by a change in temperature.

Faint Signal - This term refers to the sound characteristic of a target that may be either deeply buried or small in size.

False Signal - This term refers to a signal that appears to be an error.

Ground Balance - This term refers to using a special circuitry to cancel out the effect that iron ground metals can produce over actual metal objects.

Head - This term refers to the coil attached to the bottom of the metal detector.

Hertz - This term refers to cycles per second.

kHz - This term refers to Kilohertz or 1000 cycles per second.

Loop - This term refers to the coil or head located on the bottom of a metal detector.

Meter - This term refers to the component on the detector that offers visual information to help in identifying targets. Most metal detectors will feature either a LCD or needle indicator to display this type of information.

Mode - This term refers to an operation that used to produce desired functions.

Motion Discriminator - This term refers to a type of metal detector that requires the coil to be in motion to activate ground balance and other discrimination functions.

Pinpointing - This term refers to locating the precise location of a target regarding the center of the search coil.

Signal - This term refers to the audio response or visual indication that is received when a target is found by the metal detector.

Target - This term refers to an object that results in a visual or audio response of the metal detector.

Where to Buy this Book

You can buy this book on Amazon. Just go to amazon.com (or your local Amazon site if available) and search for **"Metal Detecting Tips by David Cardwell"**.

You can also order it at any bookstore. Just give them the IBSN below:

ISBN 978-0-9866426-2-3

CPSIA information can be obtained at www.ICGtesting.com
Printed in the USA
LVOW101732171212

312061LV00020B/703/P